SOUTHERN FRIED ROCK

The Life, Times & Music® Series

SOUTHERN FRIED ROCK

The Life, Times & Music® Series

Andrew G. Hager

FRIEDMAN/FAIRFAX
PUBLISHERS

A FRIEDMAN/FAIRFAX BOOK

ISBN 1-56799-231-5

Editor: Hallie Einhorn
Art Director: Jeff Batzli
Designer: Terry Peterson
Cover Design: Zemsky Design
Photography Editor: Emilya Naymark
Production Manager: Jeanne E. Kaufman

Grateful acknowledgment is given to authors, publishers, and photographers for permission to reprint material. Every effort has been made to determine copyright owners of photographs and illustrations. In the case of any omissions, the publishers will be pleased to make suitable acknowledgments in future editions.

Printed in the United States of America by Quebecor Printing Semline, Inc.

For bulk purchases and special sales, please contact:
Friedman/Fairfax Publishers
Attention: Sales Department
15 West 26 Street
New York, NY 10010
(212) 685-6610 FAX (212) 685-1307

website: http://www.webcom.com/~friedman/

Dedication

To the love of my life, Sarah

Acknowledgments

Special thanks to Paul Desjarlais
and to Hallie Einhorn

Contents

Introduction

While southern politicians fought against the concept of racial equality, white and black southern musicians of the twentieth century made effective strides toward the eradication of prejudice. By paying homage to the strengths of one another's musical traditions, southern musicians have embraced our commonalities and in turn tried to bring an end to political and economic barriers between races.

Nowhere in the entertainment world has the challenge to enlighten the public in regard to our constitutional commitment to equality been made more evident than in the rise of southern rock and its African-American counterpart, rhythm and blues. By the

1950s, the music performed by emerging black and white entertainers became so similar in form and content that listeners were challenged to identify the race of the performer. With the blending of their sounds, musicians had put to the test the notion of whites and blacks being inextricably different.

But as the similarities in song structure, instrumentation, and vocal style used by southern white and black musicians seemed to indicate that the wall between the races was no longer justifiable, an outraged public came to see the rocking southern music as an affront to society. Inevitably, those who felt threatened by the common links turned to the music industry to put a stop to "race-mixing."

Opposite: To this day, southern performer "Little Richard" Penniman claims to be the real king of rock. Left: With roots in country music, Bill Haley was a pioneer of rock and roll.

The industry's hasty response was an ineffective attempt to mend the eroding fence between the races. New titles for old racially motivated marketing ploys were adopted, "whitewashing" the problem in order to keep black music recordings from America's white youth. Black musicians began to be marketed under the title rhythm and blues, white musicians under the term rock and roll. Thankfully, the music emanating from America's radios was not so easily segregated. The movement toward an integrated music continued.

The rebel flag, which has so often been associated with southern rock for marketing reasons, continues to be an unrepresentative symbol of the hard work of southern musicians on either side of the color line. Although most Americans' idea of southern rock is gauged by limited knowledge of the white southern rockers of the seventies, white and black southern musicians over the last century have shared equally in the rise of this socially significant music.

Glenn Frey, along with his fellow Eagles members, contributed to the nationwide popularity of southern sounds during the seventies.

Two Types of Music in the Southern United States

Many diverse musical elements have worked together during the last two centuries to give rise to the genre that has come to be known as southern rock.

During the nation's formative years, the music performed by settlers had only the English language in common. A song's structure, its instrumentation, and the vocal quality used to portray its story were directly dependent upon the heritage of the individual musician. Music of the South was as diverse as the languages spoken in the newcomers' native lands and as the customs that the settlers brought with them to their new home.

European choir techniques are a basic part of the foundation of southern music.

The American "roots music" that evolved out of the European experience is actually the result of a combination of many Euro-tribal traditions. Europeans of common descent trekked together across the New

World and brought with them the music of their native land. Their shared musical heritage played a significant role in tying their collective past to their shared, unknown future.

As the nature of a rugged, unfamiliar continent forced these diverse European groups to work together, new songs based on a variety of European melodies began to emerge. Soon these early Euro-American songs began to find a common and uniquely American identity.

The European-derived vocal technique that became most popular over time, and which has become the prototype for many white southern singers today, is the nasal or bell-tone sound with little to no use of the vibrato. When tones such as this are used in the context of a choir, the musical illusion of a single voice in four-part harmony occurs. Both inside and outside the realm of religious music, European choir techniques became an American standard. Many singers of southern rock, from the birth of rockabilly to the present day, have their roots in this tradition.

By the 1800s, the instruments that were most commonly being used by white musicians were the piano, guitar, and fiddle, all of which have continued to be prevalent in the twentieth century. Many other instruments of European origin, such as the dulcimer, were neglected over time or replaced by newfangled instruments, such as the now popular Hawaiian-style pedal steel guitar.

The originally European fiddle is still used frequently by southern musicians.

The rhythmic traditions of African music have played a large role in the emergence of southern rock.

African-American music, too, is the product of many different traditions. Music, both religious and secular, played a large role in bringing Africans from separate tribes and languages to a common cultural ground in the Americas.

What has separated African-American musical contributions from the Caucasian-American tradition is the collective experience of four hundred years in slavery. The musical rights of slaves were, like everything else in their lives, restricted primarily to the instruments allowed them by their owners and to European-based Christian song forms. Yet from within these confines, unique African-American sounds developed.

The collaboration between blacks of different ethnic origins gave rise to several significant musical elements that would in turn play a large role in twentieth-century American music in general and, by the 1950s, the emergence of southern rock in particular. The first of these elements, the evocative African-American vocal style, with its wide array of tones, was the product of many diverse African tribal traditions. The addition of these tones to the palette of white vocal stylists began occurring in the infancy of the southern rock (or rockabilly) movement.

Another element, the indigenously African drum, which is now the centerpiece of American popular music, was not embraced by white musicians or fans until the 1930s. Similarly, the use of tones outside the major and minor scales was slow to gain acceptance and did not become a standard of white American music until the beginning of the twentieth century with the incorporation of the blue note. Although modal scales had been common in many European music traditions, they were not a standard of popular Euro-American song forms before that time.

The Impact of Changing Technologies

With the advent of recording technology in 1914 and the birth of the radio following shortly thereafter, the racial barriers between the different types of music were put to the ultimate test. Exposure to the "other" culture's music no longer required an interested party to socialize with members of the "other" race but instead could be achieved by simply

The advent of the radio made a variety of ethnic musical traditions accessible to Americans.

turning on the radio. The intracontinental communication network linking different regions and peoples of the vast North American continent began to put an end to the isolationist presumption that blacks and whites were irrevocably different.

From top to bottom: Musical innovators Louis Armstrong, Jelly Roll Morton, and W.C. Handy played crucial roles in the development of many types of popular music that depended on instrumental solos, from western swing to rockabilly.

By the 1920s, the southern-style blending of musical forms had led to an increasing number of popular music styles. Because of their unique contributions and the impact of the radio and recording industries, African-American performers such as Louis Armstrong (1900–1971), Jelly Roll Morton (1885–1941), and W.C. Handy (1873–1958), along with many others, gained international notoriety from the music that they created using European instruments.

In turn, the adoption of African instruments by southern whites brought several radio artists a great amount of popularity. The banjo, an African-American instrument consisting of steel strings over an African drum, became so popular among Caucasian radio listeners—thanks to such musicians as Uncle Dave Macon (1870–1952) of the Grand Ole Opry and southern performer Samantha Bumgarner (1880–1960)—that few are now aware of the banjo's African roots.

But it was the incorporation of the blues scale by early white recording artists that had the greatest impact on popular American music, notably southern rock. The man known as the Blue Yodeler, white southern singer and songwriter Jimmie Rodgers (1897–1933), forever changed the definition of Caucasian "roots" music. On account of his contributions, the blues became permanently subsumed into mainstream American music.

Rodgers, a fourteen-year veteran brakeman and water boy for the Ohio and Mobile railroad lines, serviced tracks to nearly every major southern city. He became a participant in the musical language of African-Americans while working side by side with first- and second-generation freedmen. This influence made him an overnight sensation when he turned to music as a profession after tuberculosis brought his early retirement from the railroad.

The blending of culturally diverse kinds of music in a southern society that was still coming to terms with a post–Civil War South resonated strongly among whites. For the first time in American history, they were working hand in hand with former slaves. Music became a cultural bond, owing to the voracious appetites of American radio and recording listeners.

Early Signs of a Rockin' Future

As the pace of industrialization became more frenetic, the music performed by southern musicians took on faster rhythms at increasingly louder volumes. Although traditionalists tried their best during the 1920s and 1930s to exclude the electric bass, electric guitar, drum, and microphone from legitimization, these instruments began shaping popular American music.

With these developments, the southern music performed by white singers and musicians began to diverge into different schools. Two of these schools, both of which took advantage of the burgeoning technology, have played a crucial role in southern rock.

The first, western swing, was a hybrid of Mexican mariachi music, the blues, Louisiana's Dixieland jazz, and, oddly enough, the Hawaiian guitar. Of these elements, the incorporation of jazz improvisational techniques had the most lasting impact on southern musicians.

Bandleader, fiddler, and businessman extraordinaire Bob Wills helped shape the nation's early twentieth-century musical impressions of the then—recently "tamed" West.

The most popular of the western swing performers, Bob Wills (1905–1975), began his career as a fiddler, playing house parties with his own band around the Fort Worth, Texas, area. After a stint at radio station WBAP, Wills landed a job with KFLZ promoting Light Crust Flour with the band the Light Crust Doughboys. (Unfortunately, his duties extended beyond the advertisement of the product to include loading and unloading the flour and delivering it to various stores in the Fort Worth area.)

Wills left the Doughboys after one of many disputes to form what became the most popular western swing band in the United States. By the year 1938, Bob Wills and the Texas Playboys had started a musical trend that raged from the East Coast to the West Coast of the United States.

The second, and most influential, school of Caucasian-performed southern music was honky-tonk. Arising after World War II, this style of music was named after a type of rowdy club usually located on the outskirts of "dry," or alcohol-free, counties. Honky-tonk made great use of the drums and electrified steel guitar. With its tawdry lyrics and groaning blues, this style of music has had the greatest influence on southern rock.

Honky-tonk's brightest star, Hank Williams, reflected the sentiments of the times in his music. The son of an incapacitated, shell-shocked World War I veteran, Hank spent most of his young life earning money by singing in the streets in order to feed himself and his mother. It was during that time that he became the student of

Hank Williams' indelible influence on the anthem style lyrics of southern rock remains a cornerstone of this type of music.

another panhandler and guitar player named Rufe Payne, known as Teetot. A blues player by trade, Teetot gave Williams the introduction to the blues that ultimately made him the most influential songwriter of his day.

Singer and songwriter Lefty Frizzell has also been acknowledged by many country and southern rock performers as one of their primary honky-tonk influences. Frizzell's hit song "If You've Got the Money, I've Got the Time" (1950) is an example of how the attitudes of southern audiences had changed by the 1950s from rural optimism to urban cynicism.

Meanwhile, African-American music was making similar strides. Around the time that western swing was gaining momentum, African-American music was also being greatly affected by technology. The invention of the microphone allowed the singer to become a significant part of the big band. Before the microphone, the singer's voice had been relegated to a small role in music since it could barely be heard over the booming brass orchestra.

The first real signs of rock and roll and rhythm and blues became apparent during this time in the music of a vivacious son of a vaudeville performer. Louis Jordan, a bandleader with a tremendous stage persona, made the first real gains toward rock and rhythm and blues by using a small brass combo (or group) to perform such rowdy hits as "Caldonia."

The incorporation of the electrified guitar and bass into African-American blues music, which began to occur in the 1930s, made a lasting impression on other types of southern music, and has become an undeniably essential element of southern rock. Bluesmen like Muddy Waters and Lightnin' Hopkins, who are regularly heralded as the greatest influences of most rock guitarists, began their rise to fame during this era.

Hank Williams (1923–1953)

From left to right: Lucretia, Hank Jr., Audrey, and Hank Williams. Despite this cheerful photo, the family was torn apart by Williams' alcohol and drug abuse.

Although Hiram "Hank" Williams was shunned by the Nashville establishment from very early on in his career, this prolific songwriter remains one of the most popular country stars of all time.

Born to Lon and Lilly Williams of Mount Olive, Alabama, Hank began to demonstrate a talent for music when he was very young. Although employed by the age of ten as a shoe shine boy and peanut vendor, Hank found enough time to learn the guitar from a local African-American bluesman known as Teetot. By the time he was eleven years old, Williams had learned the basics of the guitar and had begun writing his first songs. The following year he won first prize for "WPA Blues" at a local songwriting competition.

Soon after, Williams formed his first band, Hank Williams and the Drifting Cowboys. The group played hoedowns and square dances and even starred on their own program on radio station WSFA in Montgomery, Alabama.

After the breakup of the band, Williams became a literal drifting cowboy and made his way to Texas. He tried his hand at the rodeo, but after one solid fall off the back of a wild horse, his dream of being a cowboy was dispelled forever. The fall left him with back problems that would antagonize him for the rest of his brief life.

Williams then turned back to the profession of singing, touring the South with a medicine show. While on tour he began his torrid relationship with first wife Audrey Shepard (1923–1975). He also discovered a passion for "medicine."

Williams' days of performing were interrupted for a brief period near the end of World War II when he went to work in the shipyards of Mobile, Alabama. Once finished with this service, he swore that he was going to commit himself full-time to pursuing a career in music. He again formed a band called the Drifting Cowboys, this time with his wife "Miss Audrey" as backup singer, and began working steadily enough to gain a reputation on the circuit—as both a great showman and a drunk with a flair for missing gigs.

At the age of twenty-three, Williams had his first audition with the nationally renowned Grand Ole Opry, but his reputation unfortunately preceded him. Needless to say, Hank was not asked to be a guest on the program.

It was during this trip to Nashville, however, that Williams had his first real stroke of luck. Fred Rose, the cofounder and president of the Acuff-Rose Publishing Company, signed him to a writer's contract, ensuring that Williams' songs, if not sung by Williams himself, would be recorded and popularized by other country artists.

Rose realized that Williams, although inconsistent, was one of the finest lyricists and melody makers in the business. (Unlike the Grand Ole Opry, Rose did not have to depend on Williams to show up for anything on time.) But though he believed in Williams' talent, he was not capable of persuading the Nashville music industry to work with the unreliable singer/songwriter. So when a New York—based company named Sterling Records came inquiring about new "hillbilly" talent, Rose seized the opportunity and turned their attention toward Hank the Drifter. The company paid for a series of recording sessions at Nashville's WSM Studios that was so successful that Rose took it upon himself to become Williams' manager and began searching out a better contract with a larger label. It was not long before the newly formed MGM label, the product of Frank Walker, former president of RCA Victor and Columbia, snatched Williams out from under Sterling and launched his international career.

By 1949, Williams had become one of the most popular entertainers in American music. With the overwhelming success of "Lovesick Blues," even the Grand Ole Opry was forced to view him in a more favorable light and asked him to make a guest appearance on the show. During that stint, his performance of "Lovesick Blues" was received with six encores, an unheard of phenomenon for the then-thirty-one-year-old program. The Opry made him a "permanent" member of their company the following year.

But by 1952, the years of drinking and drug use had begun to take a whopping toll. Audrey divorced him, taking their children, Hank Randall and Lucretia, and more than half of Hank's personal assets with her. Similarly, the Grand Ole Opry could no longer accept Williams' growing substance abuse and revoked his membership. Although he quickly remarried, to singer Billie Jean Jones, his life and career were on an apparently permanent downhill spiral. On the first day of 1953, Hank Williams, only twenty-nine years old, died of a heart attack in the backseat of a sky blue Cadillac on the way to a performance. His last hit song, which was released shortly before his death, was poignantly titled, "I'll Never Make It Out of This World Alive."

In his brief lifetime, Williams wrote more than 120 well-crafted songs, thirty of which were chart-topping country hits. Sadly, all the awards that he was to receive came after his death. Along with Jimmie Rodgers and Fred Rose, Williams became one of the first three members of the Country Music Hall of Fame at its opening ceremony in 1961. The Country Music Association gave him its Pioneer Award in 1973. In 1989, the association gave him and Hank Jr. the award for Vocal Collaboration on "There's a Tear in My Beer," a song that also earned father and son a Grammy in 1990. "Your Cheatin' Heart" won a Grammy in 1983, and in 1987 Hank Sr. earned the Lifetime Achievement Award. A bronze statue of Williams now stands tall overlooking a city park in the performer's hometown of Montgomery, Alabama.

Lefty Frizzell (1928–1975)

William Orville Frizzell, otherwise known as Lefty, was a hard-drinking gambler who loved a good fight. He was also thought to be Hank Williams' only real competition for the title of greatest honky-tonk performer. But the only personal rivalry that existed between Lefty and Hank, who regularly caroused together, revolved around who could party harder.

Born March 31, 1928, in Corsicana, Texas, Frizzell spent most of his life as a performer. By the age of twelve, his professional career had begun with a regular spot on KELD radio in El Dorado, Texas. By the time he was fourteen, he was playing local dance halls and radio stations around Greenville, where he and his family had moved. By sixteen, he was a road-worn professional of the honky-tonk circuit in and around Dallas.

The first two Frizzell singles to be released nationally entered the charts one week apart in 1950. Both of these songs—"If You've Got the Money, I've Got the Time" and "I Love You a Thousand Ways"—went to number one. The following year, Lefty had seven top-ten entries on the charts, including three number one songs. He then moved to California in order to take part in the television show "Town Hall Party."

Frizzell's next success came nearly eight years later with "The Long Black Veil," which went to number six on the country charts. In 1964, he scored yet again with the memorable "Saginaw, Michigan."

His last big hit, "Falling," came in July 1975, after he left Columbia for ABC Records. That same year, a stroke, most likely brought on by high blood pressure and alcoholism, claimed his life. Besides being immortalized by his music and a place in the Country Music Hall of Fame, Frizzell lives on through a statue that stands in the center of Jester Park in Corsicana.

Louis Jordan (1908–1975)

Arkansas native Louis Jordan (above, center) gained a wealth of knowledge about music and the art of performance well before his own success as a musician. His father, a vaudeville performer, made Louis aware at a very early age that the key to being a successful musician relied as heavily upon showmanship as it did on the actual music.

By the 1940s, Jordan had begun to amass a large following with the Tympany Five, a small combo he had put together that made full use of his own vaudeville comedic style. However, it was their great songs that led the band to become the most jiving and irrepressible group in the country. Hits such as "Five Guys Named Moe," "Choo Choo Ch'boogie," and "Caldonia" heralded the beginning of a rocking American music that mixed comedic lyrics with a swinging beat.

Jordan's constant touring and never-ending quest for hit songs kept him a favorite among music fans for decades. While the works of many musicians who tried just as diligently to second-guess the desires of their listeners ended up sounding quaint or trivial, Jordan's music was just as fresh and funny at the end of his career as it had been in the beginning. Even lesser-known singles such as "Jordan for President" (with its amusing line "I promise that every living American will get his portion—after I've had mine") and "Two Little Squirrels (Nuts to You)," seem as hilarious today as they did when they were first recorded.

In the early 1990s, Jordan's music was revived in the Broadway revue *Five Guys Named Moe*, named after one of his early hits. The show, much like Jordan himself, relied unrelentingly on good tunes and laughter for laughter's sake.

Rockabilly and Rhythm and Blues

With the overwhelming success of both honky-tonk and the electrified blues, southern musicians began making a substantial amount of headway into the larger arena of pop music. The most financially successful artists on both sides of the color line continued to work toward the idea of an amalgamated American music balanced between two segregated worlds.

Southern performers came the closest to that single American sound in the 1950s. Nearly every popular song of that era, whether sung by a black or white performer, exploded with unabated showmanship and locomotive rhythms.

But the idea of placing this new American music into a single category, and thereby into the same section of record stores, was obviously impossible due to segregation in the South and continuing tensions between the races in northern urban centers. Two separate titles for the same musical phenomenon arose: rockabilly (soon known as rock and roll, thanks to disc jockey Alan Freed) and rhythm and blues (a title coined by *Billboard* magazine).

One music-production house, Sun Records, had the foresight to groom young artists whose music tested these boundaries further. If not for Sun's producer, Sam Phillips (b. 1923), and his personal mission to expand the popularity of racially mixed music, the pop culture phenomenon of rockabilly may never have occurred.

Phillips, a farmer's son born in Florence, Alabama, on January 5, 1923, began working as a disc jockey for Muscle Shoals' community radio station during his teenage years. After graduating from high school, his growing passion for engineering led him to Nashville to seek work as a radio engineer. Within only two years, he moved on to Memphis, where at the age of twenty-one he opened his first business, the Memphis Recording Service.

Phillips' young company had its first regional hit with Jackie Brenston's "Rocket 88." In 1951, on the wave of this success, Phillips

With his flashy looks and daring moves, Elvis Presley left audiences screaming for more.

founded his label Sun Records and within the first year had produced the likes of rhythm and blues performers Junior Parker, Howlin' Wolf, and Rufus Thomas.

The year 1954 brought Phillips a relationship with a young talent by the name of Elvis Presley. Presley's African-American-influenced vocal technique was risky, and the reaction from Tennessee's white population could have been grave. But instead, Elvis became an international star. Interestingly enough, it was Nashville's country music industry that ultimately brought him this vast success, when RCA bought his contract out from under the Sun label.

Both rockabilly and rhythm and blues heralded a new consensus on reality. The idea of revolution, a stepping away from the past into a new and very real other world, seemed inevitable to the young and completely dangerous to their parents. Although Elvis Presley was the first and greatest example among white performers of the changing ideology, several other southern white male singers soon followed, thanks to his welcomed arrival. Two such entertainers, Jerry Lee Lewis (b. 1935) (known to his fans as "the Killer") and Carl Perkins (b. 1932), author of "Blue Suede Shoes," brought their spectacular talents to Sun Records and in turn to the hearts of the American people.

Elvis Presley (1935–1977)

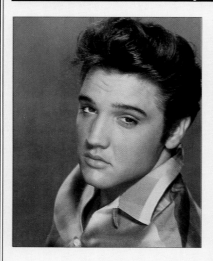

Now known to the world as the King of Rock and Roll, Elvis Aron Presley was born (along with a twin brother, Jesse Garon, who did not survive birth) to Vernon and Gladys Love Smith Presley on January 8, 1935. Elvis' birthplace in Tupelo, Mississippi, a two-room shack built by Vernon out of $180 worth of lumber, remained the family's home until 1948, when Vernon was arrested for selling moonshine and ordered by the court to leave town.

With his father in constant financial and legal straits, Elvis felt the need from a very early age to take care of his loving but often depressed mother. Their uncommon mother-son bond led many of Elvis' peers in his new hometown of Memphis, Tennessee, to refer to him as a mama's boy. Elvis spent much of his time tending to his mother, playing the guitar that she had bought him, and listening to the music of the region's popular African-American blues musicians.

It was his growing musical interest that led Elvis to wear flashy clothing. The home of the Memphis blues scene, Beale Street, and especially its locally popular "black" clothing store Lansky's became Elvis' hangout. There, he was able to become friendly with many of the local black musicians, as well as begin his outlandish clothing collection.

By his junior year of high school, the little notoriety Elvis had gained from his flashy appearance became his largest problem. His more conservative classmates regularly harassed him. Thanks to the assistance of the largest member of the high school football team, Red West, Elvis was spared any impending pummeling. Forever grateful, Presley made West his personal bodyguard for thirty years.

Although Elvis spent much of his time in high school learning the guitar and grooming his personal vocal style, he rarely performed for anyone other than his mother. It was not until after graduation that Elvis began working toward a career in music. While employed by Crown Electric, Elvis made his first recording at the now famous Memphis Recording Service. Although nothing came of that early recording, Elvis began to catch the attention of the studio's owner, Sam Phillips. Teaming up with local guitarist Scotty Moore and bassist Bill Black, Elvis was finally able to impress Phillips with his talent and begin his trek toward stardom.

The blending of country, gospel, and popular music of both black and white entertainers of the day was as dangerous to Elvis' well-being as was his clothing. Crossing over culturally in a segregated South could have had Elvis and the band run out of town—or perhaps worse. Airplay of their first single, however, proved that this type of music was to be a first step toward social integration. The response to Elvis' interpretation of the song "That's Alright Mama," by blues artist Arthur "Big Boy" Crudup, was so positive that the disc jockey who first played the single had the immediate urge to interview Elvis. By July 19, 1954, only fourteen days after the recording had been completed, the single had sold more than twenty thousand copies locally.

The Elvis craze that grew during the following two years became more than Phillips or Elvis' manager, Bob Neal, could handle. The momentum the band had taken on could take them into the national music arena, but only if their careers were handled properly.

Former carnival employee and country music manager Colonel Tom Parker spent months trying to convince Presley that he could and would make Elvis Presley an internationally recognized musician. Parker's first challenge, though, was to gain the confidence of Elvis' parents. Because Elvis was under the age of twenty-one, any contract he entered into would have to be signed by his mother or father.

Mother Gladys was not easily swayed by Parker's urgent and overly confident manner. The "colonel" had acknowledged under her casual questioning that his military title was purely honorary (it was given to him by a friend who was in the armed forces). Why, then, would he brandish the title so proudly? It also became apparent to Mama Presley, with all the talk of money, that Parker's primary concerns were not the health and welfare of her cherished child.

Vernon, a man whose professional failings and criminal record had taught him a hard lesson in caution, most likely fretted over the terms of the contract. A lifetime non-negotiable agreement in which Parker took

Elvis married Priscilla Beaulieu on May 1, 1967, and in February of the following year, their daughter, Lisa Marie, was born. The couple divorced in 1973.

twenty-five percent of everything Elvis earned must have smacked of indentured servitude. But if Parker's predictions about the money that lay ahead were accurate, the Presleys would have nothing to worry about. Finally, at the behest of Elvis himself, they signed their son's career over to the colonel.

Contract in hand, Parker swung open the doors to his newest and most aptly named enterprise: Elvis Exploitations. The subsequent twenty years would prove both Parker and Mother Gladys Presley correct. Elvis would be wealthy beyond his wildest dreams, but he would pay a steep price. As Gladys had suspected, Parker was not who he had represented himself to be. As reported in the trial brought against him after Elvis' death by the estate of Lisa Marie Presley, the colonel was actually Andreas Cornelius van Kuijk of Breda, Holland. The court found that Parker had acted out of his own personal interests, virtually bankrupting Elvis prior to his death.

Presley's personal life also suffered as fame slowly but surely led to his demise. His continuously growing drug addiction, as well as the hours he had to keep in order to avoid his fans (from five o'clock in the afternoon to five in the morning), distanced him permanently from any semblance of normal life and ultimately cost him his life.

Although there were plenty of hard times on a personal level, Presley did not, as nearly all international figures do, live to see the decline of his career. Most performers would have been greeted with contempt had they gone to the stage as Elvis did in his final year, fragile and dying. But the awareness of his inevitable death seemed to fuel an urgency in millions to see and hear the King one last time.

Presley's recordings and memorabilia have not only continued to sell after his death but have, in fact, sold better. Since 1977, the sales of Presley products have averaged $400 million a year—ten times greater than annual sales before his death.

Jerry Lee Lewis (b. 1935)

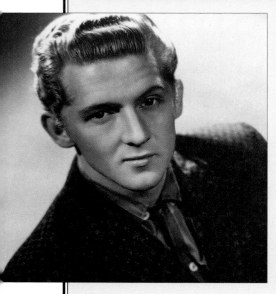

following two years, Lewis gave Sun its two greatest hits: "Whole Lot of Shakin' Goin' On" and "Great Balls of Fire."

By 1958, Lewis was giving the King a run for his money. Elvis, who had to leave the States to serve his country on a two-year stint, was worried that his career would not survive his absence. Fueling this anxiety was the possibility that Jerry Lee Lewis might replace him. Fortunately for the King, Lewis was his own worst enemy.

On the day that Lewis and his entourage landed in England for a twenty-seven-stop tour, they were met by what seemed to be the entire British media. Word had spread that Lewis had not only married

Even the most notorious of country music outlaws bowed to the ruthless behavior of "the Killer." Waylon Jennings once said of Lewis, "Just don't get too close to him and you won't get hurt." It is hard to believe that at one time Lewis wanted to become a preacher like his cousin Jimmy Swaggart. But this aspiration was thwarted when the Bible College that he attended kicked him out for his unconventional interpretation of the hymn "My God Is Real."

At the age of nine, just days before Christmas, Lewis learned to play his first song, "Silent Night." His first professional gig came five years later at the age of fourteen—just months before his first marriage. By 1950, he had begun playing regularly at the Blue Cat Night Club in Natchez, Louisiana, and had airtime every Saturday for his own twenty-minute program at WNAT radio station in the same town.

Lewis' big break came in 1956 when he was introduced to Sam Phillips, the owner of the infamous Sun Records in Memphis. The company that had only a few years before brought Elvis Presley to national attention signed Lewis. During the

The beginning of the end: Jerry Lee Lewis and cousin/wife Myra on the fateful day of their arrival in London in 1958.

a thirteen-year-old girl, but that she was his first cousin to boot. Lewis, doing himself more harm than good, tried to clear things up: "Myra and I are legally married. It was my second marriage that wasn't legal. I was a bigamist when I was sixteen. I was fourteen when I was first married. That lasted a year; then I met Jane. One day she said she was goin' to have my baby. I was real worried. Her father threatened me, and her brothers were hunting me with hide whips. So I married her just a week before my divorce from Dorothy. It was a shotgun wedding."

In the 1957 film Jamboree, *Lewis dazzled audiences with his performance of "Great Balls of Fire."*

The tour was immediately canceled and by the time Elvis returned from his tour of duty, no one, including Carl Perkins or Johnny Cash, had taken the King's throne. Lewis was down for the count.

The June 9, 1958, issue of *Billboard* magazine ran a full-page advertisement taken out by Lewis' management to address and, hopefully, dispel the cloud that loomed over his career. The ad, titled "An Open Letter to the Industry from Jerry Lee Lewis," explained that his exploits had been highly exaggerated. But the man who had been elected six months earlier by random polling in Kansas City as the real king of rock and roll (by nearly two to one) could no longer get his records played. Moreover, his performance fee had dropped from fifteen hundred to five hundred dollars a night.

The former president of the Jerry Lee Lewis Fan Club wrote about her first and only meeting with the Killer in an issue of the club newsletter. She, probably more than any other interviewer, got the clearest picture of who Lewis thought he was: "Jerry would play the piano with one hand and sing while he found what he was looking for in the Bible....Then he told us why the South lost the war...then explained the difference between a ninety-nine-year sentence and a one-hundred-year sentence."

During the course of his life, Lewis has been accused of shooting one of his bass players, killing one of his six wives, and threatening Elvis' life because the King did not believe word for word the Book of Revelation's prophecy that the end of the world was near.

Many members of the sixties' British Invasion regard Bill Haley (front, right) as the inspiration for their decision to become musicians.

The techniques of these groundbreaking rockabilly performers and their R&B counterparts were strikingly similar. The frenzied piano style and physical performances of Jerry Lee and Georgian performer Little Richard (who had a string of hits beginning with the classic "Tutti Frutti") are distinguishable only by the differing vocal vibratos of the performers and the color of their skin. Chuck Berry (b. 1926), possessed a vocal style and performed songs (such as the 1955 hit "Maybelline") that shared a great deal in common with the work of "Blue Suede Shoes" writer Carl Perkins. Perkins often recounts a conversation he once had with Berry: "Chuck said, 'We done more for the movement than any politician.' And I agree."

Other white rock performers were making headway in the music business as well. Bill Haley (1925–1981), a northerner from Michigan who was the most successful American performer to enter the British music market, and a Texan by the name of Buddy

Little Richard (b. 1935)

Richard Wayne Penniman, known as Little Richard, is heralded by many, including himself, as the true king of rock and roll. His place at the throne was usurped, many believe, for no other reason than his race. The rhythm and blues category that he found himself boxed into kept him from wider recognition. Instead of reaching the heights of megastardom by performing the material he had penned, white performers such as Pat Boone reaped millions recording and performing Little Richard's songs.

Little Richard's influence on rock performers alone is evidence of his stature in the rock music industry. David Bowie, with his effeminate persona that he called Ziggy Stardust; the Beatles, who shook their heads from side to side when singing high notes; and Elvis Presley, with the pompadour haircut, all have Penniman to thank for various aspects of their performances.

Being born in Macon, Georgia, made life treacherous for effeminate Little Richard, but at the same time it made success an imperative. Just getting by was not enough. Thanks to Specialty Records of Los Angeles, Little Richard was able to fight on a national platform for his right to life as a musician.

After a string of pop hits in 1956, which included "Long Tall Sally" and "Keep A Knockin'," Penniman was called on by Hollywood to do a number of low-budget movies. *Don't Knock the Rock*, *The Girl Can't Help It*, and *Mister Rock 'n' Roll* all paid their celluloid respects to his gregarious stage presence.

In 1957, with success under his belt and profits in his pocket, Little Richard renounced music and his lifestyle in order to follow what he believed was his real calling as a minister in the Seventh Day Adventist Church. He did not return to the music industry until 1964, when he recorded "Bama Lama Bama Loo," for Specialty. Along with Bo Diddley and the Everly Brothers, Little Richard returned to touring upon the song's release.

Since then, Little Richard has rerecorded his classic cuts in an attempt to make a comeback. He has also appeared on several nationally televised shows, singing and playing the piano.

Buddy Holly (1936–1959)

It is hard to believe that rock music, even in its infancy, was being challenged from within its own ranks to broaden its definition. But thanks to the unique offerings of a young rocker from Texas, the idea of "alternative rock" was born.

Charles Hayden Holley was born in Lubbock, Texas, on September 7, 1936. (The "e" was dropped from his last name in the mid-fifties when the tapes from his first recording session at Decca Records were mislabeled.) His rich life in music began in grade school as a student of the violin, piano, and ultimately guitar. By the time he was thirteen, he had formed his own band with friend Bob Montgomery and had begun playing in local clubs.

If the fact that two young boys were allowed to play in bars and social clubs was not odd enough, it was stranger still that the duo had begun working on a new brand of popular music. Their diverse collection of original material, combined with their homage to standard country and dance tunes, was termed by themselves—and soon thereafter by audiences—"western bop."

Allusions to Bob Wills, the father of western swing, and to the bebop movement made it apparent to everyone that Holly was not only a performer, but an innate music histo-

rian with an understanding of how the future is consistently molded from elements of our pre-existing musical heritage. Holly had not only discovered his own unique sound, but also tried to shape an entirely new movement.

Although the band's idea of reshaping American music generated a great deal of attention from local fans, their first record producer did not have the foresight to allow the bold Texas teenagers to implement their unique spin on pop-oriented music. Instead, for their first album Montgomery and Holly were persuaded to record a collection of conventional country tunes. Both in sales and in content, the album did not succeed.

Holly's first real break into the national music arena came in 1954 as an opening act for Bill Haley and the Comets, who were at the time America's most popular rock band. The following year, Decca Records persuaded Holly to drop his longtime friend and partner Montgomery for a solo recording contract.

Once again, Holly's producers restricted his musical style. Much like his debut album, which has been described as a series of sluggish singles, the follow-up met with poor sales.

With his lifelong dream still intact but his ego wounded, Holly moved back to Lubbock and began to form a new band. The result, the Crickets, was a collection of old friends: Jerry Allison on drums, Joe B. Mauldin on bass, and Niki Sullivan on lead guitar.

What the band needed was a producer who understood and trusted their unique sound enough to allow it to be pressed into vinyl. The owner of a Clovis, New Mexico, recording studio, Norman Petty, turned out to be just that person. The Crickets could finally market the music that Holly had spent thirteen years trying to promote.

With a more upbeat version of "That'll Be the Day," which had previously been recorded under Holly's Decca contract, the

Crickets received the attention of the Decca subsidiary label Brunswick, and in turn Holly finally achieved the acclaim that he so rightly deserved. In fact, the Coral recording label was so taken by the success of his work for Brunswick that it signed him to a solo recording contract outside of his work with the band.

The growing success of the Crickets meant that they had to tour almost continuously. Regardless of the size of the club or the price of the ticket, Holly's management felt that it was crucial for the band to be seen at any and all events. At times some of the bookings turned out to be big mistakes. The group found themselves occasionally mistaken for and being booked as an African-American band.

The most grueling of these mistaken musical identities was a three-night booking at the famed Apollo Theatre in Harlem. Their first two nights were an all-out failure with the band being booed off the stage. On the third and final engagement Holly stayed in good stead with the crowd by opening with a Bo Diddley song. The Crickets survived that last night without being tossed off the stage.

In the summer of 1958, Holly began negotiating with the legendary Peer International, a publishing house formed by country music mogul Ralph Peer, to publish his music. During that time, Holly began striking up conversations with the company's receptionist, and within two weeks Maria Elena Santiago had swept him off of his feet and into the wedding chapel. After their sudden marriage, the bride and groom headed to Acapulco for their honeymoon. During the trip, Holly began to reassess the direction of his career, and he came to the conclusion that his music would be better managed by someone other than Norman Petty. The members of the Crickets, though, realized that Petty's crucial investment had made them an internationally recognized group, and they fought vehemently against his release. After a series of heated arguments, Holly split from the band.

Holly's career continued to grow after the breakup. His new band, the musicians of which were considered by Holly and his label as merely backup talent, included none other than soon-to-be rising star Waylon Jennings.

By 1959, Holly and the new crew were booked on a nationally touring rock show that was headlined by other popular rock stars, including the Big Bopper (J.P. Richardson) and Ritchie Valens (singer of "La Bamba").

Although the show was a sold-out success, the legion of stars was having hard luck on the road. Within only two weeks of touring, the bus suffered a number of breakdowns. By the time the group reached Clear Lake, Iowa, many members had fallen sick and were at their wit's end over continuing transportation troubles.

Holly decided that it was best to charter a four-seater plane for his band so that they could get some rest before their next gig. But by the end of the night's performance, the members of Holly's backup band were persuaded to give up their seats on the plane for the ailing Big Bopper and an exhausted Ritchie Valens. Eight miles (12.8km) from the airport their plane crashed, killing all the passengers and the pilot.

Holly's unique singing style, rhythmic hiccup phrasing, stuttering, and teenage energy gave audiences the understanding that rock did not have to be the playground for the sexy, older-than-he-looks blues-style crooner. From Holly's perspective, the common denominator for good rock was not any specific stylizing, but the challenge of exorcizing the doldrums from rock audiences' lives.

Entire movements in rock and roll have been based on Holly's ideals—if not based entirely on his style. Many new wave musicians of the eighties drifted toward, if not outright stole, Holly's persona. And such impressive musicians as Elvis Costello and the Beatles have indicated that if there had been no Buddy, their music would have taken an entirely different route.

Holly (1936–1959) expanded the definition of rock and roll to include vocal performances more akin to the European-American singing tradition and shared a persona that was less dependent on sex appeal.

Female southern performers, too, made significant and lasting contributions to the rockabilly and R&B genres. In doing so, they effectively challenged the societal roles that have traditionally been assigned to women. Two white performers, Wanda Jackson (b. 1937), best known for her hit single, "Let's Have a Party," and Brenda Lee (b. 1945), known as "Little Miss Firecracker," nearly single-handedly brought the sexual revolution to white women.

Etta James' soulful style influenced nearly every R&B and rock singer during the sixties and seventies.

The black female performers who had begun their ascension toward equality during the big-band craze again made strides with the rise of rhythm and blues. Dinah Washington, a crossover performer who had made a healthy living in jazz before her years recording rhythm and blues, and the influential Etta James gained international popularity during the early to mid-fifties.

Wanda Jackson (b. 1937)

Although Wanda Jackson, who consistently placed in the twenties on the pop and country charts during the course of fifteen years, never made it into the top ten, her raucous, sexual rockabilly persona paved the way for future women of rock and roll.

Born in Maud, Oklahoma, on October 29, 1937, Jackson began to take an interest in music at the age of six when her father taught her the guitar. By the age of nine she was playing piano, and at age twelve she was doing daily fifteen minute (soon to be half hour) radio spots at KLPR in Oklahoma City, near her hometown of Maud. She quickly became the most popular radio personality in the region.

Around this time, she was invited by country singer Hank Thompson to tour with his band, the Brazos Valley Boys. In 1954, she got her own recording contract with Decca Records and began pumping out hits. The duet "You Can't Have My Love," featuring Jackson and Billy Gray, hit number eight on the country charts. Shortly thereafter, Jackson toured as a solo act, opening for Elvis Presley.

Jackson recalls that it was Elvis who persuaded her to become a rockabilly performer. He had stated that country-rock fusion was soon to become the rage (as it did) and that it was time to get on the bandwagon. An evening with Elvis and his collection of blues records convinced her that rockabilly was the music for her.

Unfortunately the world of music was not ready for the sexual revolution. At the Grand Ole Opry, Jackson was asked to cover her bare shoulders. (At the time, even spaghetti straps were too risqué for public viewing.) Her career suffered not from a lack of interest but the denial thereof.

But Jackson soon met with tremendous success outside the United States as she became one of the first country stars to achieve international stardom. With her screeching rendition of "Fujiyama," she became an overnight sensation in Japan. In Germany, too, with a song called "Santo Domingo," she received acknowledgment for her astounding ability.

But Jackson's achievements were not limited to her singing talents. As a songwriter she found success with Buck Owens' rendition of "Kicking Our Hearts Around" and with her own recording of "Right or Wrong," which was released in 1961. Also in the sixties, Jackson became the star of her own television series, "Music Village."

By the late sixties, Jackson had returned to more conservative country. Finally in the seventies, tired of the limitations put on her by Capitol Records, she returned to the music of her childhood, gospel, recording with MYRRH and World Records. Now with the Swedish label Tab Records, Jackson can record all types of music without limitations.

Equality, Inc.

America's struggle to uphold the Bill of Rights and its ideal that "all men are created equal" started coming to a head by the end of the 1950s. The business practices of the American music industry were beginning to be questioned regularly in courts of law. James Brown, Little Richard, and Chuck Berry began demanding restitution for the one-sided contracts given to them over the years by their white producers.

In turn, black entrepreneurs began realizing that African-Americans would not achieve true equality in the music industry until they owned the means of production. Music houses were established by African-Americans during the

Opposite: Although James Brown (top) and Chuck Berry (bottom) are now highly regarded for their significant contributions to rock and roll, their financial success was minimal due to marketing techniques that were consciously divided along racial lines. Left: Sly Stone continued to promote and produce his music during the early seventies through the white-owned rock industry, while most black performers moved to primarily African-American-owned labels.

sixties and put a halt to the notion of a single, color-blind American music. For the first time in the twentieth century, the musical demarcation along racial lines was delineated by African-Americans.

The fallout from this reevaluation was significant. Allegiance to rhythm and blues quickly turned to two new forms of music produced, performed, and written by African-Americans: funk and soul. Recording labels such as Motown and Stax Records finally gave African-American businessmen and musicians a piece of the larger financial pie.

After Chuck Berry and Little Richard, the contribution of black musicians to the idea of a color-blind American pop music became practically nonexistent. Allegiance to the ideal of an autonomous African-American identity took many performers away from the struggle to rise through the white-owned music industry. Although in the seventies Sly and the Family Stone and Jimi Hendrix came the closest to blurring the lines between rock and blues after the death of R&B, the reconsideration of the black musical identity virtually ended the twentieth-century southern musical challenge.

Physical evidence of the black contribution to southern rock (such as an African-American southern rock performer) is now almost nowhere to be found. The white men who performed southern rock during the seventies, however, attributed their sound to African-American blues and white country music.

Influenced by legendary southern-blues performers, Jimi Hendrix brought the art of playing the electric guitar to new levels.

The Leaders of Southern Rock

Although the country music industry was the first to bring performers such as Presley to international attention, the quickly changing lifestyles of musicians during the sixties ultimately pitted Nashville against the southern rocker. Long hair, flaunted drug use, and a popular disrespect

Along with the rest of the Allman Brothers Band, Gregg Allman (left), Dicky Betts (center), and Berry Oakley (right) rocked American audiences, inspiring many other bands to follow their lead.

for elders were quickly met with great disdain by Music City (how quickly Nashville's elite had forgotten the indulgences of Hank Williams and George Jones). Nashville's rejection of the next musical generation gave the rock music industry the right to call the southern hippy/hillbilly a member of its extended family. The advent of this cosmic cowboy image gave many musicians and their hometown fans a chance to let their hair down.

The Allman Brothers Band began the southern rock trend that brought dozens of southern groups to national attention and inspired many bands from outside the South to incorporate southern-style instrumentation into their sound. Gregg Allman's blues-influenced vocal style and white Tennessee drawl joined with his brother Duane's blues guitar licks to create a distinct sound that led to the upswing of a national craze by the early seventies. Aside from the incorporation of the extended rock jam into concert performances, their most influential musical contribution was their use of two lead guitars that often followed one another in duet.

Lynyrd Skynyrd, with their unique anthem-style lyrics and an Allman Brothers–influenced guitar style, were also leaders in the southern rock trend, and they became one of the most successful bands in all of rock. Initially, the lineup consisted of Ronnie Van Zant (vocals), Gary Rossington (guitar), Allen Collins (guitar), Billy Powell (keyboards), Leon Wilkeson (bass), and Bob Burns (drums). Although the band formed in 1965, their big break did not come until 1972, when they were discovered by Al Kooper, who produced their debut album *pronounced leh-nerd skin-nerd*. When recording this album, the band was joined by a third guitarist, Ed King of Strawberry Alarm Clock. From 1973 until 1977, Lynyrd Skynyrd experienced continual success on the rock and popular charts and performed a series of sellout concerts. What would seventies rock have been like without such classics as "Sweet Home Alabama" (a rebuttal to Neil Young's "Southern Man" and "Alabama") and "Free Bird" (a tribute to Duane Allman)?

A young Gregg Allman before alcoholism and drug addiction permanently damaged his nervous system.

The Allman Brothers Band

Brothers Gregg (left) and Duane Allman (right) in 1971 setting up for one of their now famous Fillmore East concerts.

Duane Allman (1946–1971) and Gregg Allman (b. 1947) gained entrance into the blues the hard way. Their childhood in Nashville, Tennessee, was tempered by poverty and the abrupt death of their father in 1958, when Duane was only twelve years old. Their mother, who could not find a means of feeding her children in their home state, soon moved the family to Daytona, Florida.

It was during these formative years in Daytona that the brothers began listening avidly to the black music stations that lined the southern coast. The emotional intensity and unique melodic structures of the blues clearly moved them both. Gregg soon took up the guitar, but ultimately turned his attention toward keyboards. He passed his guitar on to Duane along with the minimal knowledge of chord structures that he had acquired.

In 1965, the two began playing around town with their own band, the Allman Joys. Producer Bill McEuen was impressed enough with the brothers to bring them to Hollywood to record. Their work with McEuen lasted only until 1967, when they took up a recording offer with a small label. But their band, then known as Hourglass, did not fare well under the label's rules. The songs that they recorded during this period were selected from a box of taped songs from which the company demanded they choose. Moreover, the company would not permit Hourglass to play in Los Angeles clubs.

With an offer to become a studio musician for a small label called Muscle Shoals dangling before him and opportunities dwindling in California, Duane left Los Angeles for the South. Gregg stayed in Los Angeles to honor their apparently miserable contract.

Duane's work at the label brought about an introduction to drummer Butch Trucks. The duo's jam sessions proved successful enough for Duane to persuade Gregg to join him in Muscle Shoals, Alabama.

Upon Gregg's arrival, the three musicians began experimenting with material that Gregg had written but had not been able to record with Hourglass. With the inclusion of members from the band the Second Coming—Dicky Betts and Berry Oakley and drummer Jai Johanny Johanson, the Allman Brothers Band was born.

Confident that the combination of Gregg's writing and the band's unique use of dual guitars was sure to rock the charts, the band headed for New York City in the year 1969 in order to record their debut album, *The Allman Brothers Band.*

Though the album was met with only critical acclaim, the Allman Brothers were a mere two years and two albums away from national notoriety. *Live at the Fillmore East*, a collection of three double albums recorded and released in 1971, had only seven songs on each album, all of which totaled a whopping fifty-four minutes of recorded material. With the compendium's release, songs such as "Statesboro Blues," "Stormy Monday," and "Hot 'Lanta" became classics.

The Allman Brothers' notion of extended jams and the use of dueling guitars brought rock into a new era. But within a year of their successful release, the group experienced a grave setback. Duane, who has been described by the band members as the glue that held together their diverse styles and personalities, died in a motorcycle accident. In his memory, the band released *Eat a Peach*, which consisted of cuts from the Fillmore sessions as well as a new hit, "Melissa." *Brothers and Sisters*, the first album after Duane's death to consist solely of new material, was produced under the direction of Dicky Betts and brought the band the biggest hit of their career, "Ramblin' Man."

The group would again be dealt a devastating blow in 1972 with the death of bassist Berry Oakley, who, eerily enough, was also killed in a motorcycle accident. If the losses were not enough, 1974 brought a media blitz on the band members' personal lives. With Gregg's oddly timed solo career, his marriage to Cher, and a drug bust, the Allman Brothers never left the attention of gossip and news magazines. Although the band had been successful financially for the previous five years, the spending habits of the individual members forced them closer to insolvency.

The final nail in the band's coffin came at Gregg's drug trial. His testimony against road manager Scooter Herring ultimately led Herring to be sentenced to seventy-five years in prison.

"He threw Scooter away just because he didn't need him anymore," Betts told *Rolling Stone*. "And there's not one person in this band who won't tell you anything different than that. That's why there's no Allman Brothers Band....There is no way I can work with Gregg again, ever."

It took four years, apparently, for the wounds to heal. In 1979, the surviving band members reunited and recorded two records, *Reach for the Sky* and *Brothers of the Road*. Soon, however, the band called it quits for a second time.

Although Gregg scored his first hit in fifteen years in 1987 with "I'm No Angel," his solo career seemed to be coming to an end. With the twentieth anniversary of the Allman Brothers in 1989, however, there was a rebirth of interest in his work. Epic signed both Betts and Allman to a touring contract, and a multidisc compilation containing several previously unreleased tracks was produced.

Immediately following the tour, the duo began work on *Seven Tours*, which was produced by Tom Dowd. Upon its release in 1990, the album was hailed by critics as a return to the Allman Brothers' true roots.

In 1991, with their album *Shades of Two Worlds*, the Allman Brothers scored once again. Critics credited the inclusion of guitarist Warren Haynes for bringing to life the original Allman sound with his homage to Duane's guitar styling.

During these later years of collaboration, the ever-strained relations between Betts, Trucks, Allman, and Johanson seem to have finally been reconciled. "We're just taking it easy and seeing what happens from here," Trucks told a reporter from the Detroit Free Press. "[Epic producers] were afraid we would break up again before we ever finished the [anniversary] tour."

Producer Tom Dowd finished Trucks' statement. "Now they're enjoying each other's company again, and they realize how valuable they are to each other."

Ironically, the Lynyrd Skynyrd album entitled Street Survivors *was released only a few days prior to the plane crash that killed some of the band members.*

The band's tremendous success, however, was followed by tragedy. In October 1977, a plane crash claimed the lives of Van Zant, guitarist Steve Gaines (who had joined the band in 1976), Gaines' sister Cassie, and manager Dean Kilpatrick, bringing an end to the band that had been named after an Alabama gym coach. But some of the surviving members continued their contributions to rock well into the eighties by forming the Rossington Collins Band. In the late eighties, several former Skynyrd members, joined by a couple of new additions, toured together under the name Lynyrd Skynyrd. Although this "reunion" was met with little fanfare, classic Lynyrd Skynyrd tunes continue to receive a lot of airplay on rock stations across the country.

The Heyday of Hard Southern Rock

Thanks to the contributions of the Allman Brothers and Lynyrd Skynyrd, many other southern bands, whose virtuosity and contributions vary greatly, were given an opportunity to record. Throughout the seventies and into the eighties these bands rocked the charts with their blends of country, blues, soul, and rock and roll.

The Charlie Daniels Band was Nashville's means of getting in on the southern rock phenomenon. In the face of rock's tremendous popularity, Nashville's music industry regretted its initial rejection of the new breed of musician. Realizing it had misjudged the market, Nashville embarked upon a quest for acts that could fit into the new mold and that would hopefully allow Music City to regain control over southern music. With Charlie Daniels' diverse musical background, they did just that.

Charlie Daniels (b. 1936)

His work as a producer, which began in 1969 for a group called the Youngbloods, finally led him to a contract as a solo artist in 1970. Over the next nine years, he had a string of hits beginning with "Uneasy Rider." The peak of his nine-year streak was his all-time top-selling single, "The Devil Went Down to Georgia" (1979), which popularized the album *Million Mile Reflections*, sending it to platinum.

The man who challenged the devil to a fiddle contest was born in Wilmington, North Carolina, on October 28, 1936. At the age of fifteen, he took up the fiddle and within two years headed his own bluegrass band.

By 1960, his musical interests had changed dramatically, and like the times, he headed toward rock and roll. His band the Jaguars would go through several musical styles, including jazz, before Daniels adopted a rock-influenced country sound. His first hit as a songwriter, "It Hurts Me," was recorded by Elvis and was pressed as the flip side to the King's hit "Kissin' Cousins."

In 1967, Daniels was invited by a Nashville producer to work as a session musician. Within the next two years, he played on Bob Dylan's "Nashville Skyline" and on albums by other artists, including Ringo Starr and Marty Robbins.

From that pinnacle onward, Daniels and his band regained the national spotlight sporadically. In 1980, the group recorded and released "In America," a song dedicated to the hostages in Iran. Two years later, Daniels received airplay with "Still in Saigon," a memorial to America's involvement in the Vietnam War. It was not until 1988 with the release of "Boogie Woogie Fiddle Country Blues" that Daniels made it back on the charts. Two years later he scored again with the title track to his album *Simple Man*.

The Charlie Daniels Band received the Country Music Association's Instrumentalist Group of the Year award in both 1979 and 1980. These two years were big for the band, as it was during this time that they also received the Grammy for Best Country Vocal Performance by a Duo or Group for "The Devil Went Down to Georgia" and *Music City News'* Band of the Year award.

The Marshall Tucker Band was one of those groups that followed the lead of the southern rock masters Lynyrd Skynyrd and the Allman Brothers. Despite the band's title, there was no member named Marshall Tucker. (Marshall Tucker was the owner of the place in which the band practiced.) The original members—all natives of Spartanburg, South Carolina—were lead guitarist Toy Caldwell, bass player Tommy Caldwell, rhythm guitarist George McCorkle, vocalist and keyboardist Doug Gray, saxophonist and flutist Jerry Eubanks, and drummer Paul Riddle.

The band initially signed with Capricorn Records, a label whose mission was to popularize hard southern rock. From the band's inception in 1971 until 1978, most of their albums went gold or platinum. Their greatest hit was the single "Heard It in a Love Song," which oddly enough reached only number fourteen on the charts. Unlike most bands, their success was driven not by top-selling singles but rather by a loyal following who continually bought their albums.

Another successful southern rock band was the Outlaws. Formed in 1974 in Tampa, Florida, the band originally consisted of guitarists Billy Jones, Henry Paul, and Hugh Thomasson; drummer Monty Yoho; and bassist Frank O'Keefe. The group signed with Arista Records and recorded their debut album, *The Outlaws*, which was released in 1975. In that same year, they hit the charts with the memorable single "There Goes Another Love Song." Between 1975 and 1980, the band—whose members were constantly changing—pumped out at least one album a year.

The rowdy southern band Molly Hatchet—named for a murderer who beheaded her lovers after sex—emerged out of Jacksonville, Florida, in 1975. During the seventies, their lineup consisted of guitarists Dave Hlubek, Steve Holland, and Duane Holland; vocalist Danny Joe Brown; bass player Bonner Thomas; and drummer Bruce Crump. After two years of performing in the South, Molly Hatchet signed with Epic Records in 1977. The band gained their widest recognition for the single "Flirtin' With Disaster," which was the title track of their second album. In 1980, Jimmy Farrar joined the ranks, replacing

During the late seventies and early eighties, Molly Hatchet toured heavily, sometimes playing more than 250 dates per year.

Brown on vocals. The band continued to score with the public on the two albums that followed, reaching number twenty-five on the charts with *Beatin' the Odds* (1980) and hitting again with *Take No Prisoners* (1981).

Like Molly Hatchet, .38 Special arose out of Jacksonville, Florida, in 1975. Featuring twin lead guitarists and two drummers, the band released their first album under the A&M label in 1977. Although the early albums of these "wild-eyed southern boys" exuded a more "traditional" southern rock sound, the band did not achieve their first top-ten single—"Caught Up in You"—until the early eighties, when they adopted an approach more closely aligned with the pop rock music of that decade.

Black Oak Arkansas basked briefly in the southern rock limelight.

Probably the strangest group to emerge from the southern rock movement was Black Oak Arkansas. Their drug-induced ramblings were made successful primarily on account of a favorable review by a critic from *Rolling Stone* magazine who later confessed that, when he had first listened to Black Oak's record, he was stoned out of his mind. The critic received a great many angry letters from readers who had bought the album at his behest. The members of Black Oak Arkansas, who were nearly all toothless at the time of their brief heyday, quickly retreated to their Ozark home.

Other southern rockers such as Wet Willie, Elvin Bishop, and Blackfoot also made their mark on the music world. Along with their more well known counterparts, these jamming musicians helped infuse the rock scene with the sound of the South.

Southern Sounds
Outside the Southeast

California's recording industry was quick to respond to the southern rock craze. Bands formed outside the South, such as the Doobie Brothers and Creedence Clearwater Revival, wrote lyrics and music that clearly reflected southern living. CCR in particular met with huge success, performing together for an outstanding twelve years and cranking out megahits including "Proud Mary" and "Down on the Corner." By the end of the seventies many other

48

California-based bands such as the Eagles, Little Feat, Pure Prairie League (whose lead singer was Vince Gill), and the Atlanta Rhythm Section joined the trend.

One of the more unique California-based southern rock bands, the Dixie Dregs, blended fusion rock with country music. Their technical virtuosity gave southern rock a sense of respectability even among jazz aficionados whom the group regularly entertained at clubs throughout the United States and Europe.

Texas, too, contributed heavily to southern music with the success of ZZ Top and, by the mid-eighties, Stevie Ray Vaughan and the Fabulous Thunderbirds (headed by another Vaughan, brother Jimmie). As they had done since the inception of country music, Texas musicians pushed the pop music envelope by further incorporating the blues into their music.

Austin's own guitarist extraordinaire Stevie Ray Vaughan died in a plane crash in 1990, just after performing with Eric Clapton in Milwaukee, Wisconsin.

The Doobie Brothers

Two of the original members of the California band the Doobie Brothers—Tom Johnston and John Hartman—began playing biker clubs in 1969 with bass player Greg Murphy under the name Pud. When Pud disbanded, Johnston and Hartman teamed up with Dave Shogren. But it was with the inclusion of folk musician Patrick Simmons, a guitarist and singer, and Tiran Porter, who replaced Dave Shogren on bass, that the Doobie Brothers began to develop their own unique sound.

The newest members brought with them two important elements. Porter and Simmons together added second and third harmonies to Johnston's vocalizing, while folk guitarist Simmons grounded Johnston's hard rock guitar playing within the context of simpler, more memorable instrumentation. It was with the inclusion of Simmons and Porter that the band decided upon the name the Doobie Brothers, in honor of their shared appreciation for marijuana.

In 1971, only one year after deciding upon the name, the band was signed to a contract with Warner Brothers Records. Unfortunately their first album, *The Doobie Brothers*, did not fare very well. As a result, Johnston, the band's lead songwriter, took it upon himself to shift the direction of the band's sound and, he hoped, career.

The result, *Toulouse Street*, was released the following year. That album took the band and two of their songs to the top ten. "Listen to the Music" and "Jesus Is Just Alright" are to this day staples of classic rock. The Doobies would again score big with their 1973 album *The Captain and Me*, which quickly went platinum because of two more top-ten hits, "China Grove" and "Long Train Runnin'."

Determined to keep a warm place in the hearts of their fans without compromising their music, the group made at least two hundred personal appearances that year, while trying to steer away from the conventional pop-style album that they were afraid of being pigeon-holed into producing. On account of their continued creativity, the band scored big with the release of their fourth and least pop-oriented album, *What Were Once Vices Are Now Habits*. That album went platinum owing to the support of their loyal following and the biggest hit of the band's career, the number one song "Black Water."

On account of growing exhaustion from the road and continued drug use, the Doobie Brothers' membership began to change frequently. The most important roster change

Patrick Simmons (left), Tiran Porter (center), and former Steely Dan guitarist Jeff "Skunk" Baxter (right) brought to the Doobie Brothers the southern-style picking that was crucial to the band's success.

Believes," and "I Keep Forgetting" not only kept the Doobies alive, but also helped steer popular music toward the brighter, more cleanly produced sound of the eighties.

By 1980, the band had changed musicians so many times that the only original member left was Patrick Simmons. With continuous offers from big labels for Simmons and McDonald to begin solo careers, the likelihood of the band's survival seemed grim. In 1982, after two years of ignoring the inevitable demise of the Doobies, the band started their Farewell Tour.

came in 1975, when Johnston left the group because of bleeding ulcers. His replacement, singer/songwriter Michael McDonald, changed the direction of the group's core sound forever by turning away from the guitar as the central instrument. Instead, the synthesizer became the focus, ushering the band into the electronic age.

Although the change seemed drastic, the hits for the Doobies kept coming. "Takin' It to the Streets," "What a Fool

As fickle and fleeting as success in popular music can be, the Doobie Brothers continued to sell albums years after their breakup. The Doobies' success after death made them realize that the band had become legendary.

In 1987, the band reunited for a series of benefit concerts. The recording industry still believed so strongly in the group that Johnston, Simmons, Porter, and Michael Hossack signed a contract with Capitol Records. The fruit of their labor, *Cycles*, released in 1989, harkened back to the early pre-McDonald days. Although the album met with only fair success, the tour that followed led to sold-out shows in Japan, Australia, Europe, New Zealand, and back home in the United States.

With the inclusion of Michael McDonald on keyboard and vocals, the Doobies took on a more soulful sound.

The Eagles

Like most of the successful southern rock bands, the Eagles began as a collection of independent musicians who had primarily worked as backup musicians.

Singer and songwriter Jackson Browne is credited with bringing the budding band—then made up of Bernie Leadon, Don Henley, Glenn Frey, and Randy Meisner—to the attention of recording impresario David Geffen. Geffen was so taken by the group's early signs of greatness that he gave them an advance of $100,000 and a house in Colorado to polish the act.

Within a month they signed with the newly formed label Asylum, one of Geffen's brainchildren. Their first album, appropriately named *The Eagles*, became an overnight hit. Thanks in part to the single "Take It Easy," which had been cowritten by Jackson Browne, the album remained on the charts for nearly seven months. During that time, two other singles, "Witchy Woman" and "Peaceful, Easy Feeling," also hit the charts.

In 1973, the group's second album, *Desperado*, proved to be another best-seller. A concept album of sorts, it cast the band as outlaws of the Old West. Don Henley admitted to *Time* magazine, "The whole cowboy-outlaw rocker myth was a bit bogus. I don't think we really believed it; we were just trying to make an analogy. We were living outside the laws of normality."

The Eagles would again score big in 1974 with the release of the album *On the Border* and the megasuccess of the song "Best of My Love." In general, this album tended to be more of a social commentary than any of their previous work. The title track, for instance, alluded to the demise of former President Richard Nixon. Years later Don Henley said, "We [the band] weren't old enough or mature enough to make any sense out of it then." Regardless of their own personal feelings about the songs they had written, the public could not get enough of them. By the end of 1974, their first three albums were certified gold.

Although the band began having both personal and professional conflicts, their music and success continued to soar. *One of These Nights*, released in 1975, kept the band in the hearts and ears of the public with the popularity of its title track. In 1976, *Hotel California* brought the band their first Grammy for Best Pop Vocal Performance by a Duo or Group, as well as many other successful singles such as "Take It to the Limit," "New Kid in Town," and "Life in the Fast Lane." The most successful song from the album, its title track, featured the memorable guitar work of Joe Walsh, who replaced Leadon before the album was recorded. With the song and album still on the charts the following year, the Eagles would receive Grammy awards for Best Song and Best

Record. Bassist Randy Meisner, who left the group during this time, was replaced by Tim Schmit, former bass guitarist for Poco.

Two years and $800,000 later, the band finished producing their sixth album, *The Long Run*. Presales of more than two million copies certified the album as platinum by the time it reached record stores. As was expected, the Eagles put a tremendous amount of effort into making this album unique. The group moved away from both the outlaw image and political commentary. *Rolling Stone* described the record before its release as "the Eagles' weirdest." Tracks such as "Teenage Jail" and "The Disco Strangler" proved the magazine's assertion. Its "tongue in cheek" cynicism, as Henley later described it, was lost on most of the public. "Most of the humor," Henley continued, "is so dry nobody will think it's funny." The album did, however, produce one Grammy-winning single, "Heartache Tonight."

The group's last release before deciding to go their separate ways was a double-live set. One new song from the collection, "Seven Bridges Road," brought the band yet another hit.

Between 1980 and the band's eminent reunion years, individual members set out on their own lucrative solo careers. Don Henley, Glenn Frey, and Joe Walsh made their way to the top of the charts before the end of the decade.

Musicians in the field of country music later brought the band back to the attention of the American public. Travis Tritt began the trend by persuading members of the band to record one of their hits with Tritt as lead vocalist. Soon after, a number of country stars got together to perform twelve of the Eagles' songs, which were pressed onto a retrospective album.

With their music revitalized, the reassembly of the Eagles had become nearly imperative. The late 1994 release of *The Eagles Greatest Hits* took the band once again to the top of the charts. MTV seemed set on making the band a success by playing their reunion concert video performance of "Hotel California" repeatedly throughout the first three months of 1995.

Even though the group has a nearly perfect score—eight highly successful albums in a row—they never dared to describe themselves as groundbreaking. "I don't think we had any delusions that we were creating history or changing culture or anything," Henley told *Rolling Stone*. "We just wanted to do the work and be good at it and be respected by our fellow songwriters."

Don Henley (left) has had success on his own with such albums as Building the Perfect Beast *and* The End of the Innocence. *Glenn Frey's (right) solo career has included songs on the soundtracks for* Beverly Hills Cop *and* Thelma and Louise.

Little Feat

Thanks to the disintegration of Frank Zappa's band The Mothers of Invention, the southern rock movement was graced with yet another talented band, Little Feat. Originally named Country Zeke and the Freaks, the band was formed in 1970 by two former members of the Mothers, keyboardist Lowell George and bassist Roy Estrada.

George, who was well respected by the Los Angeles recording community, is the primary reason a band that had just begun to come together was immediately signed to a recording contract with Warner Brothers. While in the studio recording their first album, the band landed upon the name Little Feat, in honor of George and his tiny sneakers.

That album, which boasted the same name as the band, was hailed by *Rolling Stone* magazine as a "fine set of post-psychedelic country-influenced rock." Although the press in general was favorable to their eclectic sound—a mixture of jazz, rock, country, and pop—the radio stations across the country had a hard time deciding whether the band's sound was suitable for their format. Few of the stations seemed able to claim Little Feat's style as part of their own.

The problem with placing the band on the airwaves continued with each consecutive album. Although their 1972 release, *Sailin' Shoes,* did well in Europe, they again had a difficult time getting airplay in the United States.

It was most likely on account of this predicament that Roy Estrada left the band within the same year. With his exit came bassist Ken Gradney, as well as the inclusion of several other acclaimed studio artists. Guitarist and vocalist Paul Barrere and conga player Sam Clayton were brought together in 1973 to record the band's third album, *Dixie Chicken.* Although its hit single, for which the album was named, never reached the top ten, it remains to this day a southern rock classic.

The year 1974 brought the release of the band's fourth album, *Feats Don't Fail Me Now,* which included "Oh Atlanta." Like the other albums, though, its sales never averaged more than half a million copies. By industry standards, Little Feat was falling far short of superstardom.

With each album that followed, George began playing a smaller role. His attention turned from the Feat to his own solo career.

Little Feat founder Lowell George did not live to see the tremendous success that the band would achieve in the late eighties.

By the time the album *Down on the Farm* was set to be recorded, George's role had been pared back so much that he was only contracted to appear on one of its tracks.

Directly before its release, George died suddenly of a heart attack. With interest in the band waning and critics speculating that the band was nothing without its leader, the remaining members decided to call it quits.

But with the advent of classic rock stations, the band, strangely enough, began to sell more of their records than they had during their active years. With this resurgence in popularity, the band decided to regroup in 1988. Hayward, Payne, Gradney, Clayton, and Barrere, along with two new members—Fred Tackett and Craig Fuller—returned to the studio and began recording again.

In the two years that followed, they released *Let It Roll* and *Representing the Mambo*, both of which sold more during their initial releases than any of the band's previous albums. Hollywood, in turn, took advantage of their resurgence, incorporating Little Feat songs into two hit movies, *Pink Cadillac* and *Twins*.

With or without the presence of the band's founder, Little Feat continues to make a lasting impression on its fans. Much like the Grateful Dead, fans of the Feat continue to secure the band's place in southern rock history.

ZZ Top

Becoming and remaining the most successful southern rock band of all time is not, as the members of ZZ Top will tell you, a short-term venture. Among the three members of the band—Billy Gibbons, Frank Beard, and Dusty Hill—is an incredible ninety years of music business experience.

In 1964, at the age of fourteen, Billy Gibbons formed his first band, the Saints. In the time between that band and the Top, he played guitar for three other notable groups: the Coachmen, Billy G. and the Ten Blue Flames, and the Moving Sidewalks.

Drummer Frank Beard played for several lesser-known bands at the start of his career. He then became known among local Houston musicians as the leader of the American Blues Band, a group which backed such notable musicians as Lightnin' Hopkins, Jimmy Reed, and Freddie King.

Dusty Hill took up the bass at the age of thirteen, playing with various groups throughout his teens. Local Houston bands—The Deadbeats, Wild Lady and the Warlocks, and (thanks to Frank Beard) the American Blues Band—all boasted Hill's talents.

Recruiting for the Vietnam War caused the availability of high-quality Houston musicians to drop and forced almost every band to reorganize. Local producer Bill Ham, who had recognized Billy Gibbons' unique talent in his work with the Moving Sidewalks, decided to help the guitarist search out members for a new band. Dusty Hill and Frank Beard auditioned.

On February 10, 1970, the threesome had their first jam session. Gibbons recalled for *Guitarworld* magazine, "We started off with a shuffle in 'C' and didn't quit for a couple of hours. We decided that it was so much fun that we kept on cookin'."

At the behest of Ham, the band, who had decided upon the name ZZ Top, began a grassroots campaign to gather a loyal regional following. Instead of playing only the better-paying gigs, the group decided to take advantage of every opportunity to perform that was offered them.

After the Top had their first regional hit, "Salt Lick," on Ham's Scot label, London Records decided to sign them to a recording contract. Although their first album, appropriately titled *First Album*, was unsuccessful, it spawned a large tour throughout the South. Their second album, *Rio Grande Mud*, gave the group their second chart-topping regional hit, "Francine."

The group received their first bit of national exposure in 1972 with the help of the Rolling Stones, who asked them to open for them on that year's tour. The album that followed, *Tres Hombres*, quickly went platinum and brought the band their first national hit single, "La Grange."

In 1975, the release of *Fandango* brought yet another hit, "Blue Jean Blues," which stayed on the charts for an incredible eighty-three weeks and helped sell more than a million copies of the album. Their World Wide Texas Tour, put together to promote their 1976 album *Tejas*, finally established ZZ Top as legendary. Carved into the shape of the state of Texas, the stage for the tour was decorated with live cattle, bison, rattlesnakes, coyotes, and tarantulas. The tour, all told, brought in a whopping $11.5 million and broke all-time attendance records that had been set by the Beatles.

Long, wild beards have become the trademark look of ZZ Top.

The band took a hiatus for the following three years, while Ham tried to get them out of their contract with London Records. Gibbons, who holds an art degree from the University of Texas, spent his time off working as a board member of the Museum of Contemporary Arts and continuing to build his now enormous collection of unique guitars.

After finally being released from their previous contract, Ham brought ZZ Top to Warner Brothers. By 1979, they were back in the studio recording *Deguello*, which was hailed by critics upon its release as their best album to date.

From their next album, *El Loco*, to their present musical endeavors, the band has steadily moved away from their straight-ahead blues style toward a more electronically orchestrated sound. By the recording of *Eliminator*, they were depending heavily on the moog synthesizer in order to keep their sound close to the mainstream. The decision to do so proved effective, with the album selling more than ten million copies and remaining in the top twenty for over a year.

In 1989, the band decided to pay homage to their hero, Muddy Waters. The Muddywood Tour that followed was inspired by Gibbons' visit to the birthplace of Waters, the Stovall Plantation in Mississippi. With the help of Gibbons, who had fashioned into a guitar a plank of wood that he took from the floorboards of the shack where Waters was born, ZZ Top was able to raise money for the Delta Blues Museum in Clarksdale, Mississippi, by exhibiting for cash and finally raffling off the unusual guitar.

"For white boys playing the blues, you can only get away with it if it's amusing," Billy Gibbons once stated. The beards and the videos of strange, souped-up cars and scantily clad women are proof enough that the Top does not take itself too seriously. The philosophy that has made them so successful was once succinctly put by Gibbons—"Hey, have a good time."

Epilogue: A Future For Southern Fried Rock?

Although southern musicians have taken a backseat in the rock music market since the seventies (in part because of the success of newer markets such as heavy metal and, most recently, grunge) the essential

Former rock performers such as Carlene Carter (first cousin to the famous musical Carter family) finally found a home in country music, thanks to the industry's expansion of its format.

elements of southern rock continue to be a cornerstone of popular music. Now, much like it did with the rock and roll of the fifties, the country music industry has claimed the style of southern rock as its own. Travis Tritt, Tanya Tucker, and Carlene Carter continually pay their respects to the history of southern rock.

Three CD collections released during the early to mid-nineties have proved Nashville's claim to the shared sounds of country, blues, and rock music. By doing so, the country music industry has begun a campaign toward the popular return of southern rock.

The producers of the first of these CDs, *Rhythm, Country and Blues*, placed the most successful soul singers with country's current popular acts. Reverend Al Green shares the mike with Lyle Lovett, Clint Black with the Pointer Sisters, and Vince Gill with Gladys Knight. *Common Thread*, a retrospective of the Eagles' music, links the Eagles' southern style to its roots with the help of Tanya Tucker and Clint Black. And the most recent release of southern fried rock revisited, *Lynyrd Skynyrd Frynds*, is probably the most daring of the three releases. Country singers such as Tritt who straddle the fence between country and rock pay their respects to Skynyrd, the band that during the seventies made rock and roll (once again) a southern phenomenon.

Although the country music industry has worked hard to reclaim southern music for itself, the rock industry has put out a few notable bands whose influences are obviously linked to the great southern rockers of the seventies. The Black Crowes, in fact, claim that they spent many a drunken night at the grave of Duane Allman—no doubt out of respect for his contributions to music. Another band, Hootie and the Blowfish of South Carolina, have also adopted the southern rock tradition.

No matter which wing of the music business claims the right to southern rock, it is rightfully the music of all who write, perform, and listen to it. The worthy attempts during the last century to bring to the public a singular, color-blind music have given rise to an indigenously American form of music.

Suggested Listening

The Allman Brothers. *Eat a Peach.* Epic Records.

Armstrong, Louis. *Satchmo Forever!* MCA.

The Band. *The Last Waltz.* Warner Brothers.

Cash, Johnny. *Johnny Cash's Greatest Hits*, Volume 1. Columbia.

The Charlie Daniels Band. *Million Mile Reflections.* Epic.

Doobie Brothers. *What Were Once Vices Are Now Habits.* Warner Brothers.

Eagles. *Hotel California.* Asylum.

Holly, Buddy. "That'll Be the Day." Brunswick.

Hopkins, Lightnin'. *Lightnin' Hopkin's Double Blues.* Fantasy.

Jackson, Wanda. *Rockin' in the Country.* Rhino.

James, Etta. *Blue in the Night.* Fantasy.

Jennings, Waylon. *Wanted! The Outlaws.* RCA.

Lee, Brenda. "One Step at a Time." Decca.

Little Feat. *Sailin' Shoes.* Warner Brothers.

Little Richard. "Long Tall Sally." Specialty.

Lynyrd Skynyrd. *Lynyrd Skynrd Live.* MCA.

Morton, Jelly Roll. *Jelly & James.* Sony Masterworks.

Murphy, Michael. *Cosmic Cowboy Souvenir.* A&M.

Nelson, Willie. *Always on My Mind.* Columbia.

Presley, Elvis. *Elvis: His Life and Music.* Friedman/Fairfax.

Rodgers, Jimmie. *1933 Last Sessions.* Rounder.

Thin Lizzy. *Live and Dangerous.* Warner Brothers.

38 Special. *Special Forces.* A&M.

Tritt, Travis. *Lynyrd Skynyrd Frynds.* MCA.

Tucker, Tanya. *Rhythm, Country and Blues.* MCA.

Walker, Jerry Jeff. *The Best of Jerry Jeff Walker.* MCA.

Williams, Hank. *Hank Williams 40 Greatest Hits.* Polydor.

Wills, Bob. *The Tiffany Transcriptions*, Volume 9. Kaleidoscope.

ZZ Top. *Tres Hombres.* London Records.

Suggested Reading

Bulwack, Mary, and Robert K. Oermann. *Finding Her Own Voice: The Saga of Women in Country Music*. New York: Crown Publishers, 1993.

Dellar, Fred. *The Illustrated Encyclopedia of Country Music*. New York: Harmony Books, 1977.

Grissim, John. *Country Music: White Man's Blues*. Philadelphia: Coronet Books, 1970.

Heatley, Michael, ed. *The Ultimate Encyclopedia of Rock*. New York: Harper Perennial, 1993.

Larkin, Colin, ed. *The Guiness Encyclopedia of Popular Music*. Concise ed. Enfield, Middlesex, England: Guiness Publishing, 1993.

Malone, Bill C. *Country Music USA*. Austin, Tex.: University of Texas Press, 1964.

Nash, Alanna. *Behind Closed Doors: Talking with the Legends of Country*. New York: Knopf, 1988.

Star File Photos: © Bob Gruen: pp. 39, 56, 58; © Steve Joester: p. 47; © Pictorial Press Limited: p. 28 top; © Joe Sia: p. 41; © M. Thomas: p. 45 © Neil Zlozower: pp. 48, 50, 51 both, 54, 55

INDEX

Index